CREATIVE RECIPES FOR CHOCOLATE

a Salamander book

Published by Salamander Books Limited
LONDON • NEW YORK

Published by Salamander Books Ltd.,
129-137 York Way, London N7 9LG, United Kingdom.

ISBN 0 86101 613 0

Distributed by Hodder and Stoughton Services, PO Box 6,
Mill Road, Dunton Green, Sevenoaks, Kent TN13 2XX.

CREDITS

RECIPES BY: *Carole Handslip, Lesley Mackley, Janice Murfitt, Cecilia Norman, Sally Taylor and Carol Timperley*

PHOTOGRAPHY BY: *Sue Atkinson, David Gill, Paul Grater, and Graham Tann*

DESIGN BY: *Tim Scott*

TYPESET BY: *Maron Graphics, Wembley*

COLOUR SEPARATION BY: *P & W Graphics, Pte. Ltd.*

PRINTED IN BELGIUM BY: *Proost International Book Production, Turnhout, Belgium*

CONTENTS

MINTY CHOCOLATE MOUSSE

185g (6 oz) plain (dark) chocolate
315 ml (10 fl oz/1¼ cups) double (thick) cream
1 egg
pinch of salt
few drops peppermint essence
TO DECORATE:
mint leaves
1 small egg
caster sugar
grated chocolate

Break chocolate into small pieces and put into a a blender or food processor fitted with a metal blade.

Heat cream in a small saucepan until almost boiling. Pour over chocolate and blend for 1 minute. Add egg, salt and peppermint essence and blend for 1 minute more. Pour into individual ramekin dishes or chocolate cups and refrigerate overnight.

Wash and dry mint leaves. Lightly whisk egg white in a shallow bowl and dip in mint leaves to cover. Dip them into caster sugar, shake off any excess and leave to harden on greaseproof paper. Place on each mousse just before serving and sprinkle with grated chocolate. *Serves 4-6*

Chocolate Pears

60g (2 oz) amaretti biscuits
3-4 tablespoons Cointreau
125g (4 oz) plain (dark) chocolate
3 tablespoons strong black coffee
1 tablespoon orange juice
30 g (1 oz/6 teaspoons) butter
2 eggs, separated
4 ripe pears

Put amaretti biscuits into a bowl, pour over liqueur, then crush biscuits to rough crumbs using end of a rolling pin.

Melt chocolate with coffee and orange juice in the top of a double boiler or a bowl set over a saucepan of simmering water. When smooth, remove from heat and beat in butter and egg yolks. In a separate bowl, whisk egg whites until stiff and fold chocolate mixture into them. Set aside. Peel pears, leaving them whole with stalks intact. Hollow out core from the base and fill cavity with crumb mixture.

Stand the pears on a plate, cutting off a small slice if necessary to make them stand upright. Spoon chocolate mixture over pears to coat evenly. Chill for several hours or overnight. Transfer to individual plates using a fish slice when ready to serve. *Serves 4*

WHITE & PLAIN CHOC POTS

125 g (4 oz) white chocolate
125 g (4 oz) plain (dark) chocolate
4 eggs, separated
3 teaspoons rum
3 teaspoons Cointreau
spirals of orange peel, to decorate, if desired

Break up each type of chocolate and place in separate bowls, each over a saucepan of hand-hot water. Stir occasionally until melted and smooth. Stir 2 egg yolks into each, then add rum to dark chocolate and Cointreau to white chocolate; stir until evenly blended. In a bowl, stiffly whisk egg whites, then add ½ quantity to each of the chocolate mixtures. Fold in carefully until each mixture is evenly blended and smooth.

Place alternate spoonfuls of each mixture into 8 small glasses, or individual dishes. Leave in a cool place to set. Decorate with spirals of orange peel, if desired. *Makes 8*

Hot Chocolate Soufflé

2 tablespoons caster sugar
125 g (4 oz) plain (dark) chocolate, broken into pieces
2 tablespoons brandy or coffee
4 eggs, separated, plus 2 extra whites
icing sugar, to serve

Preheat oven to 200C (400F/Gas 6). Butter a 1 litre (32 fl oz/4 cup) soufflé dish and dust out with 1 tablespoon caster sugar. Put chocolate into a double boiler or a bowl set over a saucepan of simmering water with the brandy or coffee. Set over medium heat and stir until smooth. Take care not to overheat the chocolate or it will lose its gloss and become very thick and difficult to combine with other ingredients. Remove from heat and beat in egg yolks with remaining caster sugar. In a bowl, whisk egg whites until stiff but not dry. Fold 1 tablespoon into chocolate mixture, then scrape into egg whites and quickly fold together using a metal spoon.

Pour into prepared soufflé dish, place on a baking sheet and bake in the oven for 15-18 minutes, until risen and just set. Serve immediately, dusted with icing sugar. *Serves 4*

DARK CHOCOLATE SAUCE

185 g (6 oz) plain (dark) chocolate
125 ml (4 fl oz / ½ cup) strong black coffee or water
60g (2 oz / ¼ cup) caster sugar

Break chocolate into pieces and put in the top of a double boiler or a bowl set over a saucepan of simmering water. Add the coffee or water and sugar.

Stir over medium heat until the chocolate has melted and the sauce is smooth and creamy. Serve hot or cold. *Serves 4-6*

NOTE: Serve Dark Chocolate Sauce with any of the following recipes: Hot Chocolate Soufflé (see page 14), Rich Chocolate Ice Cream (see page 18), and Chocolate Profiteroles (see page 20). Alternatively, serve with crêpes, accompanied by single (light) cream.

RICH CHOCOLATE ICE CREAM

2 eggs plus 2 yolks
125 g (4 oz / ½ cup) caster sugar
315 ml (10 fl oz / 1¼ cups) single (light) cream
250 g (8 oz) plain (dark) chocolate, chopped
315 ml (10 fl oz / 1¼ cups) double (thick) cream
4 tablespoons dark rum

In a bowl, mix eggs, yolks and sugar together. Put single (light) cream and chocolate in a saucepan and heat gently until chocolate has melted. Stir well to blend, then bring to the boil, stirring constantly. Pour onto the egg mixture, stirring vigorously, then transfer to the top of a double boiler, or a bowl placed over a pan of boiling water. Cook, still stirring constantly, until the custard is thick enough to coat the back of the spoon. Strain into a bowl and leave to cool.

In a bowl, whip double (thick) cream and rum together until stiff, then fold into the cooled chocolate mixture. Pour into a rigid freezer-proof container, cover, seal and freeze for about 4 hours, until firm. Scoop into chilled serving dishes to serve. *Serves 6-8*

Chocolate Profiteroles

CHOUX PASTRY:

60 g (2 oz / ¼ cup) butter, cubed

75 g (2½ oz / ⅝ cup) plain flour, sifted

2 eggs, beaten

TO SERVE:

315 ml (10 fl oz / 1¼ cups) whipping cream

hot Dark Chocolate Sauce (see page 17)

Preheat oven to 200C (400F/Gas 6). Line 2 baking sheets with silicone paper. Put butter and 155 ml (5 fl oz/⅔ cup) water into a saucepan and set over a medium heat. When butter has melted, bring to boil; remove from heat. Add flour and beat until mixture leaves sides of pan. Beat in eggs gradually until mixture is smooth and shiny. Put mixture into a piping bag and pipe walnut-sized blobs onto prepared baking sheets. Bake in the oven for 20-25 minutes, until brown, puffed up and just crisp on the outside. Make a small hole in side of each profiterole; this allows steam to escape and helps keep them crisp.

Cool profiteroles on a wire rack. When ready to serve, whip cream stiffly. Enlarge hole in side of each profiterole and pipe cream into them. Serve profiteroles with the hot sauce poured over them. *Serves 4*

CHOCOLATE FONDUE

1 pineapple
1 mango
2 kiwi fruit
250 g (8 oz) strawberries
250 g (8 oz) seedless green grapes
2-3 figs (optional)
250 g (8 oz) plain (dark) chocolate, broken into pieces
155 ml (5 fl oz / ⅔ cup) double (thick) cream
6 teaspoons brandy

Peel and core pineapple; cut into cubes. Peel mango and cut into cubes. Peel kiwi fruit and cut into wedges. Cut figs into wedges. Arrange all fruit on 6 individual plates. Chill until required.

To make fondue; put chocolate and cream into fondue pot. Heat gently, stirring, until chocolate has melted. Stir in brandy; beat until smooth.

Place a fondue pot over burner to keep warm. Serve with the fruit. *Serves 6*

RICH CHOCOLATE LOG

440 g (14 oz) can condensed milk
90 g (3 oz) plain (dark) chocolate
45 g (1½ oz / 9 teaspoons) butter
500 g (1 lb) plain sponge cake, crumbled
125 g (4oz / ⅔ cup) glacé cherries, halved
45 g (1½ oz / ½ cup) walnuts, chopped
45 g (1½ oz / 3 tablespoons) stoned dates, chopped
45 g (1½ oz / 9 teaspoons) butter
60 g (2 oz / ¼ cup) caster sugar
90 g (3 oz / ½ cup) icing sugar
30 g (1 oz / ¼ cup) cocoa

Put milk, chocolate and butter in a saucepan and stir over low heat until well combined. Remove from heat. Stir cake crumbs into chocolate mixture. Stir in the cherries, walnuts and dates. Spoon mixture onto a large piece of greaseproof paper and form into a log shape. Roll up in the paper and chill overnight. Two hours before serving, unwrap roll and place on serving dish. Melt the butter in a saucepan with caster sugar and 2 tablespoons water. Bring to boiling point. Sift icing sugar and cocoa into pan and beat well. Cool, then spread over roll. Mark with a fork to give a log effect. *Serves 8-10*

CHOCOLATE WAFFLES

60 g (2 oz) butter
60 g (2 oz) plain (dark) chocolate
185 g (6 oz / 1½ cups) plain flour
3 teaspoons baking powder
30 g (1 oz / 5 teaspoons) caster sugar
2 eggs, separated
315 ml (10 fl oz / 1¼ cups) milk
melted butter

Melt butter and chocolate. Leave to cool. Sift flour and baking powder into a large bowl. Stir in sugar. Make a well in centre; drop in egg yolks and mix thoroughly. Gradually add milk, alternating with chocolate and butter mixture. Beat thoroughly. In a bowl, whisk egg whites until stiff but not dry. Fold egg whites gently into chocolate batter.

Brush a waffle iron with melted butter and heat until hot; leave on a medium heat. Pour in a little batter and close waffle iron; cook for about 1 minute on each side or until both sides of waffle are crisp and golden brown.

Serve hot with butter and honey, jam or maple syrup. These waffles are also good topped with whipped cream and a little cinnamon. *Makes about 10*

CHOCOLATE TRUFFLE CHEESECAKE

12-14 sponge fingers
6 teaspoons brandy
250 g (8 oz/1 cup) cream cheese
250 ml (8 fl oz/1 cup) double (thick) cream
few drops vanilla essence
350 g (12 oz) plain (dark) chocolate, melted
2 egg whites, stiffly whisked
60 g (2 oz) milk chocolate, melted
60 g (2 oz) white chocolate, melted
rose leaves
1 teaspoon cocoa powder

Line the base of an 18 cm (7 in) springform cake tin with non-stick paper. Arrange sponge fingers over base. Spoon over brandy. Beat together cream cheese and cream until thick; stir in vanilla essence and cooled chocolate and mix well. Fold in egg whites. Spoon into prepared tin, level the top and chill for at least 6 hours.

For the decoration, brush melted chocolate onto underside of rose leaves using a fine paintbrush. Place chocolate side up on non-stick paper and allow to set. Repeat and leave to dry. Peel away from paper.

Arrange chocolate leaves over the top. Using a fine sieve, dust cocoa powder around outside top edge. *Serves 6-10*

BRANDY ALEXANDER PIE

250 g (8 oz/2 cups) plain flour, sifted
155 g (5 oz) unsalted butter
3 tablespoons icing sugar, sifted
1 egg yolk, beaten with 2 tablespoons water
4½ teaspoons gelatine
155 ml (5 fl oz/⅔ cup) double strength hot black coffee
3 eggs, separated
60 g (2 oz/¼ cup) caster sugar
3 tablespoons brandy
155 ml (5 fl oz/⅔ cup) double (thick) cream, whipped
60 g (2 oz) plain (dark) chocolate, melted
Chocolate Caraque, to decorate

In a bowl, rub butter in flour then stir in icing sugar. Stir in beaten egg yolk. Knead lightly. Cover and chill for 30 minutes. Preheat the oven to 200C (400F/Gas 6). Line a deep 23 cm (9 in) flan tin with pastry. Bake blind for 10 minutes. Lower temperature to 180C (350F/Gas 4) and bake for 15-20 minutes. Cool. Dissolve gelatine over the hot coffee. In a bowl, whisk together egg yolks and caster sugar until pale and thick. Stir in coffee and brandy. In another bowl, whisk egg whites until soft peaks form. Fold cream into coffee mixture. Fold in egg whites. Turn into flan case and chill for 2-3 hours. *Serves 8*

CHOCOLATE CHRISTMAS PUDDING

60 g (2 oz / 1/3 cup) glacé pineapple, roughly chopped
60 g (2 oz / 1/3 cup) glacé cherries, chopped
60 g (2 oz / 1/3 cup) raisins
3 tablespoons brandy
3 tablespoons single (light) cream
375 g (12 oz) plain (dark) chocolate, in pieces
125 g (4 oz / 1/2 cup) cream cheese
125 g (4 oz) ratafia biscuits, in pieces
125 ml (4 fl oz / 1/2 cup) whipping cream and
2-3 tablespoons grated plain (dark) chocolate, to serve

Grease a 940 ml (30 fl oz / 3¾ cup) pudding bowl. Put pineapple, cherries and raisins in a bowl; pour over brandy.

Put single (light) cream and chocolate in a saucepan and heat very gently until melted. Stir until smooth, add fruit with brandy and leave to cool. In a bowl, beat cream cheese with a little of the chocolate mixture until smooth, then mix in remaining chocolate mixture. Mix in ratafias and pour into prepared pudding bowl; chill overnight.

To serve, turn out onto a chilled plate. Lightly whip whipping cream. Pour some over the pudding and let it trickle down the sides; serve the rest separately. Decorate pudding with grated chocolate. *Serves 10-12*

MOCHA RUM TORTE

3 eggs
140 g (4½ oz / ½ cup + 1 tablespoon) caster sugar
90 g (3 oz / ¾ cup) plain flour
375 g (12 oz) mascarpone cheese, beaten
4 egg yolks
125 g (4 oz / ½ cup) caster sugar
2 tablespoons rum
2 egg whites, stiffly whisked
185 ml (6 fl oz / ¾ cup) black coffee and
60 g (2 oz) plain (dark) chocolate, grated, to finish

To make cake, preheat oven to 180C (350F/Gas 4). Grease and line a 20 cm (8 in) round cake tin. In a bowl, whisk eggs and sugar together until thick and light. Sift flour over mixture, then fold in gently. Spoon mixture into prepared tin and bake in the oven for 30 minutes, until golden. Cool on a wire rack. To make filling, in a bowl, whisk egg yolks and sugar until thick and light. Stir in mascarpone and rum. Fold egg whites into cheese mixture. Cut cake horizontally into 3 layers. Put one layer on a serving plate. Sprinkle with one third of the coffee. Cover with one third of the filling. Repeat layers, finishing with a topping of cheese mixture. Chill overnight. Sprinkle with grated chocolate to serve. *Serves 8*

MOCHA BROWNIES

125 g (4 oz) plain (dark) chocolate
60 g (2 oz) unsalted butter
185 g (6 oz/1 cup) dark soft brown sugar
2 eggs
1 tablespoon instant coffee granules dissolved in
1 tablespoon hot water
90 g (3 oz/¾ cup) plain flour
½ teaspoon baking powder
pinch of salt
60 g (2 oz/½ cup) walnuts, chopped

Preheat oven to 180C (350F/Gas 4). Grease and line a 20.5 cm (8 in) square cake tin.

Melt chocolate and butter together in a pan over low heat; set aside to cool.

In a bowl, beat sugar and eggs together until thick and pale. Fold in chocolate and cooled coffee and mix thoroughly. Sift in flour, baking powder and salt and lightly fold into mixture; then fold in nuts. Pour mixture into prepared tin and bake in the oven for 25-30 minutes, until firm and a skewer inserted into the centre comes out clean. Leave to cool in the tin for 30 minutes. Cut into squares to serve. *Makes 16*

Pains au Chocolat

250 g (8 oz/2 cups) strong white bread flour
1 teaspoon salt
2 teaspoons 'easy blend' dried yeast
185 ml (6 fl oz/¾ cup) milk
30 g (1 oz/5 teaspoons) caster sugar
1 tablespoon oil
100 g (3½ oz) butter
90 g (3 oz) plain (dark) chocolate chips
1 egg yolk and 4 teaspoons milk, to glaze

Sift flour and salt into a bowl. Stir in yeast. Make well in centre. In a saucepan, heat milk to blood heat. Combine sugar and oil. Add to flour; mix well. Knead until smooth. Put dough in a large bowl, cover and leave to rise for 1-2 hours. Repeat. Knead, then roll into a rectangle. Divide butter into three. Dot one portion over top two-thirds of dough. Fold lower third up and top third down; sealing with a rolling pin. Give dough a half turn and repeat process 3 times. Put dough into oiled polythene bag and chill for 1 hour. Cut dough in small rectangles. Sprinkle chocolate chips along short end of each rectangle. Roll up. Place rolls on a buttered baking sheet to rise. Preheat oven to 220C (425F/Gas 7). Glaze and bake for 15-20 minutes. *Makes 8*

HAND-MADE CHOCOLATES

90 g (3 oz) ready-to-roll fondant icing
rose and violet flavourings
pink and mauve food colourings
60 g (2 oz) white marzipan
6 maraschino cherries
6 crème de menthe cherries
6 whole almonds
185 g (6 oz) plain (dark) chocolate, melted
185 g (6 oz) white chocolate, melted
185 g (6 oz) milk chocolate, melted
crystallised rose and violet petals

Cut fondant into 2: flavour ½ with rose flavouring and colour pale pink. Flavour remaining piece with violet flavouring and colour pale mauve. Roll out to 1 cm (½ in) thickness and cut into shapes using cocktail cutters. Place on a non-stick paper-lined baking sheet. Shape marzipan into various shapes. Arrange on baking sheet. Dry overnight. Pat cherries dry. Toast nuts until golden brown. Using a dipping fork, coat centres with chocolate and place on a paper-lined baking sheet. Leave plain, or decorate with piped chocolate. Decorate rose and violet centres with crystallised petals. *Makes about 30*

MOCHA TIA MARIA TRUFFLES

250 g (8 oz) plain (dark) chocolate, in pieces
2 egg yolks
30 g (1 oz) unsalted butter
2 teaspoons Tia Maria
6 teaspoons double (thick) cream
2 teaspoons instant coffee powder
90 g (3 oz) plain (dark) or white chocolate, melted, for coating

Melt chocolate in a bowl placed over a pan of hot water; stir until smooth. Add egg yolks, butter, Tia Maria, cream and coffee powder and stir until mixture is thick. Remove bowl from pan, leave to cool, then chill until firm enough to handle.

Scoop out teaspoonfuls of chocolate mixture and roll into balls. Dip into melted chocolate to coat and use a palette knife to create a rough surface. Allow to set on a wire rack.

Store in the refrigerator. Use within 2-3 days. *Makes 14-16*

CHOCOLATE LIÈGEOIS

280 g (9 oz/1¼ cups) caster sugar
90 g (3 oz/¾ cup) cocoa powder

TO SERVE:
milk (see below)
vanilla ice cream
whipped cream
sifted cocoa powder for sprinkling

In a saucepan, heat sugar with 315 ml (10 fl oz/1¼ cups) water until sugar has dissolved. Bring to boil; boil for 3 minutes, stirring occasionally. Whisk in cocoa and continue whisking over moderate heat until smooth. Leave to cool, then keep syrup in refrigerator until required.

For each Chocolate Liègeois serving whisk together 250 ml (8 fl oz/1 cup) milk and 9 teaspoons chilled chocolate syrup.

Pour into a chilled glass, float a scoop of ice cream on the chocolate milk and top with a generous spoonful of whipped cream. Sprinkle with a little cocoa and serve immediately. *Makes 375 g (12 oz/2 cups) syrup*